GROWING OLD GRATEFULLY

William J. Byron, SJ

Paulist Press
New York / Mahwah, NJ

Cover image by Marek Mierzejewski / Shutterstock.com
Cover design by Kate Myer
Book design by Lynn Else

Library of Congress Cataloging-in-Publication Data
Names: Byron, William J., 1927- author.
Title: Growing old gratefully / William J. Byron.
Description: New York : Paulist Press, 2018.
Identifiers: LCCN 2017038968 (print) | LCCN 2018011048 (ebook) | ISBN 9781587687471 (ebook) | ISBN 9780809153732 (pbk. : alk. paper)
Subjects: LCSH: Older Christians—Religious life. | Gratitude—Religious aspects—Christianity. | Catholics—Religious life.
Classification: LCC BV4580 (ebook) | LCC BV4580 .B97 2018 (print) | DDC 248.8/5—dc23
LC record available at https://lccn.loc.gov/2017038968

ISBN 978-0-8091-5373-2 (paperback)
ISBN 978-1-58768-747-1 (e-book)

Published by Paulist Press
997 Macarthur Boulevard
Mahwah, New Jersey 07430

www.paulistpress.com

Printed and bound in the
United States of America

To Charlie Shreiner
a friend since college days
who encouraged me to write

Contents

Introduction

The idea for this book originated on Memorial Day, May 25, 2015, when it was my privilege to begin leading a retreat for "senior priests" at the Continuing Formation Center of St. Mary's Seminary and University in Baltimore. I established my credentials to lead the group by announcing that that day was my 88th birthday.

I may well have been the most senior of the dozen men who came from Arlington, Virginia; Baltimore, Maryland; Brooklyn, New York; Camden, New Jersey; and Raleigh, North Carolina for five days of prayer and reflection together. Most were retired from active ministry; all had lived through decades of remarkable change in the Catholic Church.

"Growing Old Gratefully" became our theme as we took a cue from a small book by Jesuit Father John LaFarge, *Reflections on Growing Old: Thoughts for Turning the Latter Years into the Best Years of Life* (1962).

Father LaFarge, who was 82 when he wrote his book, saw old age as a gift, "a very precious gift, not a calamity; since it is a gift," he said, "I thank God for it daily."

We adopted that outlook and attended prayerfully to the idea of gratitude. An attitude of gratitude sets the tone of all that unfolds in the following pages. This book, of course, is intended for a far wider audience than senior priests. All elders—men and women, lay or religious, even those with no faith commitment at all—will find encouragement in these pages. Women especially will be attracted to this book. There are more women than men in the elder years; they also, I suspect, tend to read more than men do as the years go by. Anyone who has attained senior status has time to read. Spending some of that time mulling over the ideas presented here will help them find meaning that lies within their reach and is waiting to be discovered.

In his poem, *Rabbi Ben Ezra*, Robert Browning wrote,

> "Grow old along with me!
> The best is yet to be,
> The last of life, for which the first was made:
> Our times are in His hand
> Who saith 'A whole I planned,
> Youth shows but half; trust God: see all, nor
>   be afraid.'"

"The best is yet to be." Even more reason to be grateful! And now as I pass my 90th birthday, I am more than grateful to invite readers who qualify to grow old gratefully with me. As you page through this book, make note of the many persons, events, and blessings in your own lives for which you now can be nothing but grateful.

Chapter 3 invites you to "Live by the Spirit." Outlined there is an "infrastructure" for a personal spirituality. In an earlier book, *Parish Leadership: Principles and Perspectives*, I apply the same infrastructure in a modified way to the organization and operation of parish life. It is applicable to any workplace where persons of faith meet and mingle. It is surely worth including here.

1

Growing Old

Its approach is gradual. Often, you don't even see it coming, although signals are regularly sent by clock and calendar, by memory lapses, an occasional stumble, and by truth-stretching friends who keep telling you how great you look. Aging is always in process. The "life begins at" starting line keeps getting pushed back from 40, to 50, and then to 60, until the "senior" vocabulary—as in *senior citizen* and *senior moment*— paves over the cobblestone path that leads into old age. Its approach is indeed gradual and its arrival, presuming it can be marked with precision, seldom draws a standing ovation.

Old age is more than just the accumulation of years or a pile of wealth and property. Old age is a stage of life, a rank in relationship with family and friends, and, best of all, it is a gift. Only the giver of life—God—

can give it, and grateful is all that the recipient of this gift can be, which we examine more closely in the next chapter.

Back in 1961, Jesuit Father John LaFarge, a senior editor at *America* magazine, published an article titled, "On Turning Seventy" (November 18, 1961, 242–45). In it, he remarked that old age "can be a time of harvest, of selection and wisdom, with wonderful compensations all its own." And, he continued:

> The latter years are a time when we simply allow ourselves to become more familiar with God and with His saints in heaven. We should let ourselves grow closer to that source of life, that ocean of love, toward which we are inexorably moving, just as the water-borne traveler on a great river begins to scent the first tang of the mighty sea to which the current is noiselessly carrying him. It means talking much to God: to our Father in heaven, to His Son, our Redeemer, to the Holy Spirit, who is our invisible and ever-working companion, and to Christ's Blessed Mother Mary. (242)

Allow yourself to draw closer to God. Think of yourself as a water-borne traveler and think of the river of life as carrying you into the sea of God's immensity. Talk much to God, but listen too—especially to the Holy Spirit, your "invisible and ever-working companion."

Father Theodore M. Hesburgh, CSC, the longtime president of the University of Notre Dame who died on February 26, 2015, at age 97, grew old gratefully and in companionship with the Holy Spirit. His devotion to the Holy Spirit was printed on the last page of the wake program distributed to the thousands who paid their respects in the Basilica of the Sacred Heart on campus the day before his funeral Mass:

> The Holy Spirit is the light and strength of my life, for which I am eternally grateful. My best daily prayer, apart from the Mass and Breviary, continues to be simply, "Come, Holy Spirit." No better prayer, no better results: much light and much strength.

In the *America* article referred to earlier, John LaFarge wrote, "These latter years are a time for *listening*, listening to that Voice which could not make itself heard so well in the clamor of busier years. Now that voice begins to converse with us in the cool of the evening speaking to us of what it all means and what we should really be thinking of" (243). He also makes a case for the latter years to be a time of conversation with the young as well as for quiet, even "hidden" acts of charity. He notes that this stage of life is a time for courage in the face of diminution and asserts, at the end of the article, that "old age is pre-eminently a time of reparation" (245).

I was a young priest assigned to be a summer editor at *America* in 1962 and had the opportunity to discuss this article with Father LaFarge. When he mentioned reparation to me, he hastened to add that it was important not to doubt for a moment that God's forgiveness had been given and received, but it was also important to recognize that reparation "is God's gift to us time-bound mortals." The elder years simply provide the opportunity to unite all the limitations and disappointments that accompany diminishment with the sufferings of Jesus for the salvation of the world. Participation in that repair work is part of the privilege of old age.

It is indeed a privilege to be old, even though those occupying that favored status may not notice an abundance of respect, attention, and special attention coming their way. The opposite may well be the case—inattention, neglect, and simply being forgotten. The person who is old can resist all this by accepting his or her age as a fact and facing that fact every day with faith, hope, and gratitude. And I will make a point here, to be repeated throughout this book, that a person cannot be simultaneously grateful and unhappy. If unhappiness is troubling you, give gratitude a chance. You have so much for which you can and should be grateful.

2

Gratitude

Gratitude is prototypically a Catholic characteristic. It is not only central to our Catholic identity, but also an essential component to any successful plan to accommodate old age. Consider this question: How would you describe who and what we are as Catholics in one word?

If I were pressed to reduce the entire meaning of religion to one word, that word would be *gratitude*. The case for making that one word *love* instead of *gratitude* is worth attempting, but I recall learning from the First Letter of John that it was God who first loved us, thus enabling us to love—by his good gift of love—and therefore all we can be is grateful. Why? Because he first loved us; he graced us. "In this is love, not that we loved God but that he loved us and sent his Son to be the atoning sacrifice for our sins" (1 John 4:10).

We are also reminded that the old American vernacular used to express gratitude by simply saying, "Much obliged." Obligation under God springs from a sense of gratitude. Acknowledge gratitude as your only stance before God, and you notice the presence of moral obligation to do or not do certain things that God wants you to do or avoid.

Gilbert Keith Chesterton had something profound in mind when he wrote, "Thanks are the highest form of thought; and…gratitude is happiness doubled by wonder." I'm not altogether sure what he meant by that, but it sure sounds good! And if I were to tease out that notion, I could imagine a scenario where one is caught up in wonder, say, at the beauty of creation; or as one experiences a sense of silent wonder in the presence of God, and the mood or feeling associated with that experience is simply and purely one of gratitude.

There is a multiplier effect associated with gratitude, and the wonder of it all is that gratitude can, if you let it stretch your mind, magnify your happiness.

I once knew a small-time politician who was constantly being bothered by people looking for jobs in city government. "Six people want the job," he told me, "you give it to one and wind up with one ingrate and five enemies." Success and security can make ingrates of us all. That's more than a bit strange, but nonetheless true. Perhaps it is saying something about self and selfishness, or it may simply be spelling out a lesson in human nature. Human nature does have an insular, self-enclosing, self-interested tendency. Perhaps that relates to the survival instinct. But human nature is also social and relational; outward reaching, needing to link and bond. But will human nature share—naturally? Not easily and perhaps not naturally, but it would be simply erroneous to contend that sharing is unnatural when human happiness depends on it. So, we have to learn to share. And we learn through various stages of growth and the development of our sense of gratitude.

What stage of growth are you in now? The closer you get to open and generous sharing, the clearer the signal you are sending to others that gratitude is driving your decisions. And as you move into the elder years in your stage in life, you will notice that the years are happy in direct proportion to the level of gratitude that accompanies them.

There are stages in your moral development too, in your degree of growth in gratitude, in showing yourself to be "much obliged." Where are you now? The higher you rise above a childish "avoid getting caught" morality to a principled "doing the right thing" stage—doing it regardless of who notices and without consideration of any reward except knowing that you did the right thing—the more refined your sense of gratitude becomes.

In any case, gratitude is the ground of moral obligation, and being grateful is the best way of declaring your dependency on God. Count your blessings and be thankful. St. Ignatius of Loyola, founder of the Jesuit Order, once remarked that he saw ingratitude as the root of all sinfulness.

A contemporary Jesuit, Father Tim Brown, is the first who brought to my attention that a grateful person cannot be sad. His point is that gratitude and unhappiness cannot coexist in the same person at the same time. So, if you are unhappy, take a moment to check your gratitude quotient. You may be suffering from a serious gratitude deficit that will, upon examination, explain your unhappiness. This is a frequent problem for older people.

It is important to think about gratitude, even pray about it. Toward the end of my book *A Book of Quiet Prayer*, you'll find these words designed to serve as a starter for any reflective person thinking about giving thanks to God:

> I could start counting now, Lord,
> and I would be at it for days taking
>   inventory of your blessings to me.
> Forgive me for not noticing them more
>   readily and more often.
> When everything is going well, I rarely think
>   of pausing to say thanks.
> That's simply wrong of me and terribly
>   immature.

Now that I am taking a moment to think
    about it,
I'm beginning to notice the arrogance in my
    refusal to say thanks
and the selfishness of putting myself on
    center stage
without a nod to playwright, producer, and
    supporting cast,
not to mention the folks who built the
    theater and sold the tickets.
Let me shun for this brief moment the
    spotlight I crave
in order to find the humility I need.
And there, on the ruins of my self-
    centeredness,
I pray for an abiding sense of gratitude. One
    word turns my heart to you: *Gratias*!

Recently, I helped a man prepare for death. He
was a successful editor and author. He was battling ter-
minal cancer at age 71. He asked me to sit down and
talk to him about it—what would it be like? How do
you say goodbye? How could he make it less sad and
difficult for his wife? He reminded me that he was a
reporter and wanted to "cover" his own story, and asked
if I would mind if he recorded our conversation.

One thing that struck him in that conversation, he
later told me, was the central religious significance of

gratitude for the believer. I had said to him something like, "Just let yourself repeat the word *gratias*, breathe it in and out. Say it to God, of course, but say it to those around you too." And I suggested that he think of *gratias* as a blanket that he could pull up and around him there in bed. "Wrap yourself in thanks," I said. And he did, so that he could die gratefully even if, like most of us, he wasn't altogether grateful to be dying.

A well-known quote attributed to Albert Schweitzer states, "Sometimes our light goes out but is blown into flame by another human being. Each of us owes deepest thanks to those who have rekindled this light."

That is a most constructive exercise—good for the soul as well as for human relations: "to think with deep gratitude of those who have rekindled the flame within us." I always tell students who are applying for college, graduate, or professional school not to fail to mention in their personal essays those others (usually elders)—teachers, coaches, mentors, relatives, friends—who helped them along the way—lifted their sights; challenged them to use their talents; perhaps even lighted the flame when fear or discouragement had set in.

I underscore that point by telling them what a member of the admissions committee at a front-ranking law school told me. She would read the personal essay first and if there was no mention of anyone other than the applicant, that is, no mention of a role model, a sacrificing parent, a helpful coach or teacher, then she would set the application aside because, as she told me, she didn't want to add more self-centered people to a profession that already had more than enough self-interested, self-enclosed members in its ranks.

Before taking a gratitude walk over the past years, let me tell you one more story about gratitude. It goes back many years to a summer Sunday when I was working at Fordham University in the Bronx in New York City. I took the train from Fordham Road to White Plains to visit with friends. They would meet me at the station in White Plains and take me to their home for the afternoon and evening. When I arrived, I walked along the station and noticed a man that you might call a "drifter," or "hobo," or, as we used to say, a "knight of the road." He was sitting on a bench inside the station, and our eyes met briefly as I passed by. I greeted him with a simple "hello" and went outside. A few moments later, I noticed him approaching me. I instinctively reached into my pocket for some change, but he waved that off and said, "No, I don't want any money; I just want to thank you. You're the first person who has said anything to me in the last two days!"

Even when you are down on your luck and have very little, you can still say thanks!

Now, as you review the past years, there should be plenty of gratitude prompts. First, be grateful for the gift of life and grace. Be thankful for the gift of faith and then list the many reasons you have for being grateful.

Let's shift gears here for a moment, although at the end of this brief excursion we shall be back on the notion of gratitude.

On the Sunday before Pope Benedict XVI arrived in the United States in April 2008, the *Philadelphia Inquirer* ran a positive editorial of welcome and took the occasion to raise an interesting question: "What does it mean to be a Catholic in the U.S. today?" I'd like to ask that question here and invite you to think with me toward an answer.

All Catholics should be reflecting on that question all the time—individually, to be sure, but also with others. It is an important question and the range of possible answers is wide. None of us can say it all, but each of us should try to form a reasonably concise reply.

For me, being a Catholic today in the United States means being a person of commitment within a community.

The community, of course, is the church, with the pope as leader, teacher, and symbol of unity. But within the church, we find ourselves in other communities. There is the conjugal community for so many (marriage and the family). There are celibate religious communities for some, and there are those who remain single but still belong to families and relate to others in a variety of helping relationships.

Countless Catholics identify with other communities in their workplaces and in leisure hours where they are known as Catholic and where they witness to the truths of their Catholic faith. Aging Catholics, as indicated earlier, have more time for prayer, and they should be using that time to listen to what God might want to share with them. Listening may be an unfamiliar form of prayer, but the elder years provide time for some practice.

The commitment associated with being a Catholic (remember, I said that being Catholic means being a person of commitment within a community) is, first and foremost, to Jesus Christ. We are Christians. Catholic life is christocentric. It is both nourished and celebrated in the Eucharist. The community within which this commitment is most evident is a worshipping community that remembers the Lord in the breaking of the bread (see Acts 20). Being Catholic means being part of all that through both word (Scripture) and sacrament (Catholics count seven of these). Being Catholic also means having special reverence and respect for Mary because she is the mother of Jesus.

Scripture introduces the Catholic to law (the Ten Commandments as well as the law of love). Scripture, as proclamation, invites the response of faith. And Catholic faith, in search of deeper understanding, applies intellect to the content of Scripture in the exercise of Catholic theology. Theology attempts explanation, as contrasted with proclamation, and therefore develops new understandings (the development of doctrine) over the years. Hence being a Catholic means being lifted through life on the wings of both faith and reason.

Being Catholic also means being committed to the care of those in need. Those three *c*'s—commitment, community, and care—indicate what it means to be a Catholic today.

Certainly, to be a Catholic means to be with and for the poor. It means to promote peace and justice, to protect and respect human life from conception to natural death, and to care for the earth. Stewardship, in the Catholic view, extends to the care and cultivation of one's personal gifts of body and mind.

For Catholics, sexuality is to be expressed within the context of (1) community (marriage and family, and preparation for both) and (2) permanent commitment (fidelity). Sexual pleasure is purposeful in keeping with God's plan for procreation. Similarly, material possessions are to be managed within the context of community (ownership may be private but use is common) as well as commitment (to stewardship, service, and the good of others).

Being Catholic means having freedom, responsibility, and accountability—freedom in the Holy Spirit, responsibility for one's free choices, and accountability for one's actions and the use of one's talents. A reflective reading of Scripture reminds the Catholic that (1) "you will know the truth, and the truth will make you free" (John 8:32); (2) that each is indeed his or her "brother's [and sister's] keeper" (Gen 4:9); and (3) that all of us will have to give an account before God in keeping with the judgment scene portrayed in Matthew 25. Earlier in Matthew's Gospel (5:1–12), the Beatitudes provide a summary of Catholic convictions, which we will discuss later.

Finally, to be a Catholic means to live in gratitude for all God's gifts, a gratitude that provides a firm foundation for moral obligation. We present ourselves as "much obliged" (grateful) before God on Sundays. And on all seven days of the week, we consider ourselves obliged as well to love one another as Christ has loved us.

3

Living by the Spirit

In his Letter to the Galatians, Paul addresses people who are converts from paganism. He instructs them in the exercise of their newly found freedom in the Holy Spirit and urges them to "live by the Spirit" in their normal secular surroundings—an appropriate phrase to direct us in growing old gratefully.

How can a person know whether he or she is "guided by the Spirit" in everyday life—at home, at work, in retirement, on vacation? In Galatians, Paul offers us some criteria for judging the consistency of one's own (or anyone else's) behavior with the presence of the Spirit in our life. They constitute what Paul calls the "fruit" of the Spirit: love, joy, peace, patience, kindness, generosity, faithfulness, gentleness, and self-control (Gal 5:22–23).

Examine what happens in daily life against these

criteria. These are nonmarket values that can humanize any place you happen to be—the marketplace, workplace, recreation area, home. All nine of these Pauline characteristics are within the reach of normal people leading ordinary lives. All nine are particularly important to a believer in the elder years.

In contrast to these ingredients of a faith-based spirituality rooted in Christian revelation, Paul mentions the "works of the flesh," that is, human activity only, activity not informed by God's indwelling Spirit. The works of the flesh are what we are left with when we reject the Spirit and set out blindly on our own. These rebel elements are "obvious," Paul notes, and he identifies them as: "fornication, impurity, licentiousness, idolatry, sorcery, enmities, strife, jealousy, anger, quarrels, dissensions, factions, envy, drunkenness, carousing, and things like these." He then states bluntly, "I am warning you, as I warned you before: those who do such things will not inherit the kingdom of God" (Gal 5:19–21).

After examining Paul's second list, some people in midlife and midcareer might be forgiven for saying, "Well, orgies aside, that's actually a pretty fair description of the setting where I spend my day." It really is not, but the description is sometimes close enough to the mark to motivate reflective persons to give the first list of positive Pauline values a closer look. And those who no longer inhabit the workplace can find evidence in their present surroundings of the disvalues that Paul had in mind.

If Christian spirituality is to mean anything at all in daily life, the Pauline criteria signaling the presence of the Holy Spirit should be the very infrastructure for any Christian's circumstance or stage in life. They should be guiding principles, pillars that support our daily life. Once internalized, these can serve as answers from within—from mind, soul, and spirit—answers to challenges to one's faith raised by circumstances in any area of life.

Representing as they do the presence of the Holy Spirit, Paul's criteria can both protect and transform a person, who, once transformed, can transform the surrounding world.

Sober reflection on the absence in oneself or one's surroundings of these positive criteria can be unsettling, as can the realization of the occasional presence of what Paul listed as negatives (especially his reference to "enmities, strife, jealousy, anger, quarrels, dissensions, factions, envy"). These experiences should be unsettling. Welcome the discomfort that can serve as an eviction notice on the complacency that stifles both the Spirit and the spirituality waiting to energize the person of faith.

Some faith-work study groups that I've encountered speak of the "Spirituality of Collaboration," which reminds me of the book *Transforming the Way We Work:*

The Power of the Collaborative Workplace (American Management Association, 1995). In the preface, the author, Edward M. Marshall, raises two questions that have special relevance here when applied to the workplace. He asks, "What would the world of work be like if we all truly respected one another?" and, "How effective would our workplaces be if we all knew how to collaborate?"

The essence of Marshall's message, which is applicable in retirement as well as in the active years, can be summarized:

> The new realities in business require a new type of leadership. Command-and-control no longer applies. Collaborative leadership, however, requires a significant shift in our relationships in the workplace. Since leadership is no longer a position but a function, and since everyone can be a leader, the responsibility for leading the organization shifts to the entire workforce. The traditional roles and responsibilities of leadership also change—from commanding to coaching, from telling to engaging, and from delegating to others to working with others. Our behaviors must change as we learn how to function in an environment of consensus formation, conflict resolution, and full responsibility." (p. 86)

If spirituality is to mean anything at all for a believer in everyday life, the criteria set out by St. Paul—signaling the presence of the Holy Spirit—must become the infrastructure we carry within ourselves in daily life. They should be both pillars and principles that support the believer's entire life. They can transform a person, who along with others similarly transformed can transform any place they happen to be.

It might be helpful to reflect on the expression "in the spirit" found in 1 Peter 3:18. "He was put to death in the flesh, but made alive in the spirit." This is not a direct reference to the Holy Spirit, but it is a reference to existence in the spirit, hence to spirituality. And for us who live a "fleshy existence" all the days of our lives, the Pauline criteria for discerning the presence of the Holy Spirit point the way to leading a spiritual life while still in the flesh. They quite literally show us the way.

Let's consider more closely the nine spiritual principles:

Love. The word means many things to many people. Popular culture debases it in song and story; great literature and great lives display its profound beauty. Essentially, love is sacrifice. It is the willingness to lay down one's life for another.

Joy. Not to be confused with pleasure or hilarity, joy is another profound reality.

Those who confuse the "pursuit of happiness" with the pursuit of pleasure, will find lasting joy always eluding them. Joy is an inner assurance that your will is aligned with God's will, that you are favored—graced and gifted—beyond anything that you could merit on your own. Joy is balance, an abiding contentment.

Peace. Often mistaken for whatever it is that follows a truce, peace is tranquility. St. Thomas Aquinas described it as the "tranquility of right order." Those who "bury the hatchet" and retain their grudges are not at peace. Those who retain their emotional balance and agree to disagree can live in harmony.

Patience. This word literally means "suffer." The agent acts; the patient receives the action. How the person receives the action, especially the unwelcome action, whatever the source—dentist's drill, honking horn, fist pounding on the table, vocal contradiction, unmerited rebuke—is the test of patience.

Kindness. It is sometimes remarked that "kindness can be cruelty." This means that weakness or timidity have slipped into virtue's clothing and are providing cover for an escape from responsibility. Kindness is respect for human dignity in every circumstance of life; it is both courtesy and courageous attentiveness displayed toward another person.

Generosity. The opposite of all that is small, closed, petty, ungiving, and unforgiving, generosity points to largeness of soul. Generosity does not come naturally to human nature weakened, as it is, by the fall of Adam. But generosity can be learned by observation and acquired by practice. Whenever practiced, it demonstrates the truth of the dictum that virtue is its own reward.

Faithfulness. Dependability and reliability are the prerequisites of friendship. Keeping commitments, commonly thought of as "promises" and theologically understood as "covenants," are the "stuff" of faith. For the believer, faith is the habit of entrusting oneself to God. In daily life, faithfulness is friendship, trust, and the security derived from commitments kept.

Gentleness. This word means different things to different people. Lee Iacocca was referred to once by a speaker at a black-tie dinner in New York as a "gentle" man (aren't all who attend such functions "ladies and gentlemen"?). Donald Trump followed the speaker to present an award to Iacocca and ridiculed the suggestion that there was anything at all "gentle" about the then chairman of Chrysler. Gentleness is so often confused with timidity that we are caught in a cultural confusion over the meaning of the word and the place of gentleness in the workplace. Gentleness is strength. The gentle person is neither insecure nor arrogant; he or she is self-possessed, in quiet control of self and the surrounding situation.

Self-Control. This test of personal integrity involves the practice of saying no to self. "Teach him he must deny himself," was the response General Robert E. Lee gave to a young mother who held up her infant son in the confederate General's presence and asked for a "blessing." A person "out of control" in matters large or small, is a diminished person. To have "lost it" in any circumstance of life, is to have abdicated that which makes one human; it is to have invited a curse and rejected a blessing.

Anyone seriously concerned with the challenge of changing life negatives into faith-based positives might well begin with this nine-point checklist, making it an instrument of daily self-examination. These nine pillars can support a personal spirituality for anyone anywhere. A practical spirituality can become personal—part of you—if you simply follow this suggestion: Write them down as a nine-point checklist in scorecard style. Reflect on them prayerfully for a few moments in the morning as you ask God's blessing on your day. Then, in the evening, again in a few moments of reflective prayer, review your checklist and mark your slippage or progress on each point as you give thanks to God for all the gifts that are yours at the close of another day. It is simple: a morning and evening expression of gratitude accompanied by a checklist review.

Before your day begins and at the end of the day before going to bed, compose yourself for a few stock-taking moments of prayer that follow a similar pattern to this (allowing for your own formulation of questions and selection of points for emphasis):

A. Recall that you are in God's presence and thank God for the gift of life and any other gifts that come to mind.

B. Ask for light to see yourself as God sees you, to see your day in the light of eternity.

C. Review your role in the day just unfolding, or just ending, against these norms:

1. Love
Morning: Am I prepared to share, serve, sacrifice for others today?
Evening: Did I share personally with others? Did I hurt anyone or hold back?

2. Joy

Morning: Is my will aligned with God's? Do I cherish the graces, the gifts of God to me? Do I recognize the difference between pleasure and happiness? Am I in balance?

Evening: Where did I turn in on myself today? When and why did sadness touch me today? Did I lose balance?

3. Peace

Morning: What image of tranquility can I carry with me into this new day?

Evening: Why was I upset? What grudges am I carrying? Did I disturb the peace of others? Did I make anyone angry?

4. Patience

Morning: Am I prepared to suffer today, if God wills it or is willing to permit it?

Evening: When and why did I "lose it" today? Did I overreact? Why did I lose my temper? Do I really believe that everything depends on me?

5. Kindness

Morning: Am I prepared to be considerate today? Will courtesy and civility accompany me through the day and will attentiveness mark my relationship to others?

Evening: Did I contribute any rudeness, abrupt demands, or insults to the rubble of this day?

6. Generosity
Morning: What will I be today, a giver or a taker?
Evening: Was I petty, ungiving, or unforgiving in any way today? Did meanness enter the world today through me? Did I make anyone smile?

7. Faithfulness
Morning: If God is God, he cannot be anything but faithful to me today and always. I resolve to remain faithful to God today and, with God's help, to keep all my commitments in faith and friendship, in dependability and reliability.
Evening: Was anyone let down by me today? Did I lose any faith in God or in myself? Did I violate any trusts?

8. Gentleness
Morning: I am capable of being rude, rough, and domineering. I want to be gentle. I hope the source of all gentleness will work through me today.
Evening: Was I harsh toward anyone today? Did I hurt anyone in any way?

9. Self-Control
Morning: I may have to say no to myself today; am I ready?
Evening: Did I leave any room for others today? Was I selfish or indulgent in ways

that diminished the world's supply of human dignity?

D. Again, give thanks and, as needed, express not just regret but resolve to make amends.

As noted earlier, reorganize these criteria in score-card fashion for your own purposes. Blank spaces can be provided on that scorecard for your own personal progress reports to yourself. One item or another on the list of nine may call for special attention at a given stage in your life; you can highlight any category you like. You can also add other criteria that suit your purposes.

Note also that the idea of gratitude underlies all nine criteria presented here in this chapter. You are, in fact, growing old gratefully!

4

Blessed Are They

D r. Frank Sweeney was a friend of mine from high school. He was in military service in World War II and then enrolled at the University of Virginia and went on to study medicine at Thomas Jefferson Medical College in Philadelphia.

Frank later became executive vice president of Jefferson and was the administrator of the Jefferson hospital. At a relatively early age, Frank's first wife, Helen, whom I knew well during our high school years, died, as did Jack McShea, another member of "our crowd," who left a widow, Mary Therese, or "MT" as we always called her, another member of that original high school circle of friends.

Frank Sweeney and MT subsequently married, blending their families in a suburb of Philadelphia while spending summers "down the shore," as we used to say, in Avalon, New Jersey. Sadly, Frank became terminally ill with cancer at age 64 and was an occupant of the VIP suite in the new hospital building that he built at Jefferson when I visited him there one summer Monday morning after spending the weekend in Avalon with many of Frank's friends. Having celebrated Mass together—Frank's friends and I—the previous morning at the home of Bob and Martie Gillin, we prayed, of course, for our dying friend Frank.

When I stood by Frank's hospital bedside and told him about the Mass in Avalon, I reminded him that whenever we pray for anyone who is seriously ill, we are always asking, in effect, for more time. "But inevitably," I said, "the answer to that prayer is going to be, 'No, no more time, but how about eternity?'" And Frank's immediate response was, "My bags are packed."

Two weeks later, Frank died and MT asked me to celebrate his funeral Mass and give the homily. As I always do, I asked the family to select the texts from Scripture to be read at the funeral and MT selected the Beatitudes for the Gospel reading. As I was preparing the homily, Frank's words "my bags are packed" kept repeating themselves in my memory and I asked myself, "What do you pack for that final journey home to heaven? It has to be the stuff of the Beatitudes!" So, I had help from Frank in writing his own funeral homily.

In the Gospel of Matthew, you find an account of this teaching of Jesus that presents a summary of what it means to be a Christian, even though at that point in history there were no Christians, nor was there a Catholic Church:

> When Jesus saw the crowds, he went up the mountain; and after he sat down, his disciples came to him. Then he began to speak, and taught them, saying:
>
> "Blessed are the poor in spirit, for theirs is the kingdom of heaven.
>
> "Blessed are those who mourn, for they will be comforted.
>
> "Blessed are the meek, for they will inherit the earth.
>
> "Blessed are those who hunger and thirst for righteousness, for they will be filled.
>
> "Blessed are the merciful, for they will receive mercy.
>
> "Blessed are the pure in heart, for they will see God.
>
> "Blessed are the peacemakers, for they will be called children of God.
>
> "Blessed are those who are persecuted for righteousness' sake, for theirs is the kingdom of heaven.
>
> "Blessed are you when people revile you and persecute you and utter all kinds of evil against you falsely on my account. Rejoice and

be glad, for your reward is great in heaven, for in the same way they persecuted the prophets who were before you." (Matt 5:1–12)

These are the so-called Beatitudes—happiness qualities, blessings, although it takes faith to see the happiness, to welcome them as blessings in your life. There are eight categories: (1) the poor in spirit; (2) those who mourn; (3) the meek; (4) those who hunger and thirst for justice; (5) the merciful; (6) the purposeful and single-hearted; (7) the peacemakers; and (8) the persecuted.

A shorter and even more countercultural version appears in the Gospel of Luke:

He came down with them and stood on a level place, with a great crowd of his disciples and a great multitude of people from all Judea, Jerusalem, and the coast of Tyre and Sidon. They had come to hear him and to be healed of their diseases; and those who were troubled with unclean spirits were cured. And all in the crowd were trying to touch him, for power came out from him and healed all of them.

Then he looked up at his disciples and said:
"Blessed are you who are poor,
for yours is the kingdom of God.

"Blessed are you who are hungry now,
   for you will be filled.
"Blessed are you who weep now,
   for you will laugh.
"Blessed are you when people hate you, and when they exclude you, revile you, and defame you on account of the Son of Man. Rejoice in that day and leap for joy, for surely your reward is great in heaven; for that is what their ancestors did to the prophets." (Luke 6:17–23)

The words here speak simply and starkly of the poor, the hungry, the weeping, the hated, the excluded, and insulted. Note that Luke says poor, not poor in spirit.

During presidential election campaigns in the United States, there is usually much discussion about how Catholics should vote and how the candidates align with Catholic teaching, values, principles, and ideals. My suggestion is to stand the candidates and their party platforms against the Beatitudes to see how well they measure up. There is no perfect match, of course, but this doesn't mean that the exercise is futile. It reminds us that the core message of Christianity is summarized in the Beatitudes. So, put yourself in that crowd, fix your eyes on Christ, and listen intently.

Blessed are the poor in spirit. Jesus teaches a healthy detachment here; urging those who would follow him not to be possessed by their possessions; to fix their hearts on higher things and not get caught in the trappings of wealth.

Blessed are those who mourn. Mourning is a part of life, as we all know. But so is the comfort that only God can give and that only the faithful heart can know.

Blessed are the meek. Meekness is not weakness; never confuse timidity with humility. True humility is courage. Christian meekness is uncommon courage, the courage of the cross.

Blessed are those who hunger and thirst for righteousness. Righteousness, or justice, is fairness. It involves the protection and promotion of just relationships. It is truly God's work.

Blessed are the merciful. Firm, but gentle; shrewd, but ever forgiving; that's how you temper justice with mercy in imitation of the just man who first articulated these Beatitudes.

Blessed are the pure in heart. This praises the single-hearted, the person of integrity, and it delivers a promise that all of us hope for—to see God, as Jesus promised we would, if only we are just. That's the reward of single-heartedness, of being clean and clear of heart, of being the opposite of the double-minded man.

Blessed are the peacemakers. We all must be reconcilers, dispute resolvers, mediators. We are each called to contribute to the cause of peace. If we do, peace will be ours forever.

Blessed are those who are persecuted for righteousness' sake. To some extent, this "persecution" can and will happen to all of us. No one can go through life without encountering some misunderstanding, unfair treatment, underappreciation, and occasional recrimination. That's what it means to be a disciple, a follower, an imitator of Christ.

Blessed are you when people revile you and persecute you and utter all kinds of evil against you falsely on my account. To the extent that any of this comes your way in the line of duty, so to speak, on the path of Christian discipleship, so much the loss for the persecutors and so much the gain, the eternal gain, for you.

Rejoice and be glad, for your reward is great in heaven. And that says it all! There you have the "stuff" of the Beatitudes. That's what Frank Sweeney had packed for his trip home to heaven. He didn't have to worry about weight limits or the number of carry-ons; in his daily sojourn through life, he just had to attend to the important things, like not being possessed by his possessions, being single-hearted, being merciful, humble, compassionate, just, a peacemaker.

St. Leo the Great was a pope who died in 461. He once gave a sermon on the Beatitudes in which he said, "When our Lord Jesus Christ was preaching the Gospel of the kingdom and healing various illnesses throughout the whole of Galilee, the fame of his mighty works spread into all of Syria, and great crowds from all parts of

Judea flocked to the heavenly physician." And then Leo pointed out that those who were to be instructed in the divine message "had first to be aroused by bodily benefits and visible miracle so that, once they had experienced his gracious power, they would no longer doubt his doctrine." In other words, the miracles Jesus performed got their attention, but "in order to cure men's souls now that he had healed their bodies, our Lord…climbed to the solitude of a neighboring mountain, and called the apostles to himself" (Sermon 95, 1–2, PL 54:461–62).

Leo suggests a parallel between this mountain of the Sermon on the Mount, and Mount Sinai where the Lord met Moses and gave him the Ten Commandments. The message to Moses, said Pope Leo, "evidenced a terrifying justice." But now, the words in Jesus's Sermon on the Mount "reveal a sacred compassion." It is, says Leo, a "tranquil discourse." Listen again to Leo the Great: "Concerning the content of Christ's teaching, his own sacred words bear witness; thus whoever longs to attain eternal blessedness can now recognize the steps that lead to that high happiness."

The steps, of course, are the eight Beatitudes. They lead you home to heaven. And with each step you take, your gratitude grows accordingly.

5

A Grain of Wheat

In *Reflections on Growing Old: Thoughts for Turning the Later Years into the Best Years of Life*, John LaFarge writes,

> The great fact of old age, no matter how you look at it, is diminishment in one form or another. So the question recurs: Why is life as I now know it, as it affects me in my present existence, such a curiously diminishing thing? Why must I change so much? Why must I grow weak, why do I have to resign from occupations? Why do I find myself becoming confused, forgetting names and misaddressing envelopes? What, on the other hand, is the meaning of so many of the finer things of my latter existence? Why do I

clearly see now many perspectives and relationships that carried no patent meaning for
me in earlier days? (p. 26)

These questions led LaFarge to explore further
the puzzle of "growth through diminishment." As
he explains, "My interpretation of old age does not
rest upon a gamble, however noble. It views old age
rather as a time of life which exemplifies in countless
ways a great principle of our existence: the principle
of growth-through-diminishment" (p. 28). And he
explores this mystery through the agricultural imagery
employed centuries ago by Jesus, namely, the mystery
of the grain of wheat: "Very truly, I tell you, unless a
grain of wheat falls into the earth and dies, it remains
just a single grain; but if it dies, it bears much fruit"
(John 12:24). As LaFarge explains, "A certain decay or
death is needed for the seed to come in contact with
the life-giving forces, the various acids and alkalis in the
soil. Growth through diminishment, factually, is a law
of nature's organic system of existence as we know it.
But the *meaning* of the law is derived from the new life
that is released from the decay, the new life that is the
principle of growth" (p. 29).

The power of the growth-through-diminishment
principle, according to LaFarge, "does not arise from
some mysterious or mystical excellence which would
attach to 'diminishment' as such, for what is negative in

its nature remains merely negative. Its power relies upon something altogether different; it rests upon the sworn word of the all-powerful Creator, who has given us a hope, a firm and unshaken hope. The strength of old age lies in the firmness of that hope; we cannot understand the meaning of age unless we explore the meaning of hope itself" (p. 33). To grow old gratefully, therefore, we must be men and women of hope. LaFarge adds a helpful comment here for those whose hopes seem to slip away with the accumulation of years: "The death of old hopes allows new hopes to arise" (p. 33).

Reassuring are the words of the prophet Jeremiah: "Blessed are those who trust in the LORD, / whose trust is the LORD" (17:7). Jeremiah doesn't say one's hope is *in* the Lord (that's where his trust is), rather one's hope *is* the Lord. This identification of hope and the Lord is a point to be pondered as the aging process proceeds. If you are walking with the Lord, you are walking in hope. "Aging in a world of hope," says LaFarge, "is a totally different affair from growing old in a world, in a community, in a network of family relationships poisoned by the bitter and unnatural atmosphere of despair" (p. 40).

The poet George Herbert expressed the encouraging idea that anyone "who walks in hope dances without music." Most of us make it through life without the benefit of background music. Whether you walk or dance, you make your way each day by even-paced measures without the tempo-enhancing encourage-ment of violins and trumpets. For many years, you have probably been absorbing from the movies lessons about life that are cleverly (and often deceptively) wrapped in background music. Characters in films have music to intensify their emotional highs, warn them (and the audience) of impending danger, or accelerate their slide into deeper despair. In those rare moments of emotional intensity when the music stops, you, the viewer, are left in a suspended state of watching and waiting, trying (often uncomfortably) to figure things out for yourself.

Real life is different. You can make your own movies, so to speak, by imagining what, and why, and how you will do what you are going to do today and in all your tomorrows. But you have to choose the attitude—the inner silent state of mind—that will accompany you (and serve as your "accompaniment") along the way. If you want to walk in hope, you must choose to do so.

Hope is one of three "theological virtues," so named because each has God for its direct object. The other two are faith and charity. The object of each is God. Your faith is directed toward God; your hope is grounded in God; your charity (love) is aimed directly at God.

Your practice of these three virtues will have indi-rect effects on many other people. In consequence of your firm faith in God, you know how to be faithful to others. Full of unshakable hope that God's promises to you will be fulfilled, you can present yourself to others as a hopeful person, an anchor, a rock. Your unconditional love of God, for God's own goodness and not for what he has to give to you, enables you to convey something of the divine goodness to others in your own (by definition limited) acts of charity and love.

The one-act play *Hope Is the Thing with Feathers* has intrigued me since I first came across it in my college years. The play is a mixture of humor and pathos revolving around hobos trying to snatch a duck from a pond in New York City's Central Park. The suggestion in the title is, I imagine, that hope can flutter and fly away. Hope will flee only if you choose not to hang on to it. "I don't think hope ever dies," psychiatrist David Morrison once remarked to me; "it is buried in many people, but it can surface again."

Hope is not to be confused with optimism, which focuses always on "the best." "Optimizing" opportunities and achieving "optimal" outcomes might be "optimistically" regarded as part of "the best" in the "best of all worlds." That is not the way it is with hope. Hope is a great deal closer to the human heart—hesitant or stout, weak or strong—and to the ground on which the have-a-heart person walks (or dances!).

Hope is inextricably bound up with expectation, and, of course, your expectations will often focus on things getting better than they are right now. This is not to suggest that hope comes into play only when things are bad. You don't have to be ill in order to get better. The situation does not have to be in a deplorable state in order to begin to improve. Expectation is the thrilling dimension of hope. Expectation is part of the stretch that is integral to your spirituality, especially as you grow older.

I have no idea when the word *hopefully* rose to the prominent place of misapplication that it now enjoys in the American vernacular. That adverb means "in a happily expectant way." If used correctly, it would describe a personal condition such as the mood conveyed in expressions like "proudly announce," or "gladly welcome." The misapplied *hopefully* (as in, "Hopefully, we will hear from them soon") really means, "It is to be hoped that...."

This is more than a simple grammatical quibble. Most of the people I hear punctuating their conversations with the word *hopefully* do not give that much evidence of being all that hopeful!

The famous words from Dante's *Inferno* appear (figuratively) above the entrance to many workplaces; at least they are written on the minds of many as they go to work: "Abandon hope, all ye who enter here." They also find their way over the imaginary threshold into old age. This is not the stuff of a sound and robust spirituality capable of sustaining you on the journey.

Give yourself an "expectations check-up" from time to time, to make sure that your supply, your savings account, of positive hopes is abundant. What were your hopes, your expectations when you started out on your career? Achievement, money, fame, power, security, influence, creativity, satisfaction, the opportunity to serve, the chance to make your mark? All or some combination of the above? If you are like most other humans, few, if any, of your goals have been fully realized. There's nothing unusual about this; it is all part of the human predicament.

How, then, do you cope in the latter years? How do you keep your expectations high and positive? How do you keep yourself in balance and on course into the future?

Hope is the only route to take. Remember, hope is a theological virtue; its object is God. Forge that link for yourself in prayer and everything else will fall into line.

As John LaFarge explained, "In old age...you become much less of a record of what you have once been by your (bygone) efforts, as (you are now) a record of what the Creator is working out within you" (p. 84). It takes faith to see that something worthwhile is "working out" now in your advanced years.

Annexed to the Jesuit community in which I now live at St. Joseph's University in Philadelphia is Manresa Hall, an infirmary serving the needs of elderly Jesuits of the Maryland Province. It is my privilege to celebrate

Mass for these men once or twice each week in the infirmary's spacious sunroom. On occasion, I remind these men that Manresa Hall is a powerhouse for the Province; grace is generated there through them that support the active ministries of their Jesuit brothers throughout the Province. Others—younger, healthier, and more energetic—are doing the preaching, teaching, and sacramental ministries "out there in the apostolates," as we say, but the grace reaching the souls of those served in the various apostolates is being generated right there in Manresa Hall, just as the electricity powering the place is being generated miles away in an unknown power plant. Hence, the analogy justifying the description of Manresa Hall as a "powerhouse." Because God is pleased with these men and their lives, good things are happening elsewhere—because of them. Accepting that in faith gives these men abundant reason to be grateful. And they have more reason to say, with the poet Robert Browning,

> Grow old along with me!
> The best is yet to be,
> The last of life for which the first was made:
> Our times are in His hand
> Who saith, "A whole I planned,
> Youth shows but half; trust God: see all, nor
>   be afraid."

That message is delivered by the grain of wheat falling into the ground—"the best is yet to be." Those words become a faith-based conviction in the mind of the believer and thus reinforce the ground for gratitude in the heart of the believer. No room for regret; no reason to be sad. All the reason in the world to be grateful.

6

Adversity along
the Way

Not long ago, an out-of-work executive called me for advice. His job search was going nowhere. His divorce had just been finalized. His battle for weekly visitation rights to his only son was bogged down in red tape and made even more painful because his son didn't really care about seeing him.

This man told me that he wanted to develop a deeper sense of spirituality. He had become convinced that "organized religion is for people who are afraid of going to hell, but spirituality is for those who have already been there." He is a very good and decent person. Why, he wanted to know, were all the negatives piling up on him? He was aware that both age and misfortune were closing in on him, and he realized he needed help.

Rabbi Harold S. Kushner's wise, warm, and wonderful book *When Bad Things Happen to Good People* addresses just such difficult questions. It is written from the heart of a deeply religious man who has himself encountered great adversity in life. Kushner's son Aaron was diagnosed in infancy as having a condition called progeria, "rapid aging." The rabbi learned that his son would never grow much beyond three-feet tall or have any hair on his head or body. The boy would have the appearance of a little old man. And he would die in his early teens.

Rabbi Kushner spoke of his son in the introduction to the volume. "This is his book," Kushner wrote, "because any attempt to make sense of the world's pain and evil will be judged a success or failure based on whether it offers an acceptable explanation of why he and we had to undergo what we did." Two of Kushner's chapter titles reflect questions that are part of the human predicament: "Why Do the Righteous Suffer?" and "What Good, Then, Is Religion?"

These questions are on the minds of most thinking people in the face of human tragedy, and remain unexpressed by many. It is important for one's spiritual and mental health not only to bring these and related questions to the forefront of consciousness, but to talk them over with trusted friends. It is also important to recognize that these questions can be answered only in the vocabulary of spirituality, as indeed Rabbi Kushner demonstrates toward the end of his book:

> Let me suggest that the bad things that happen to us in our lives do not have a meaning when they happen to us. They do not happen for any good reason which would cause us to accept them willingly. But we can give them a meaning. We can redeem these tragedies from senselessness by imposing meaning on them. The question we should be asking is not, "Why did this happen to me? What did I do to deserve this?" That is really an unanswerable, pointless question. A better question would be "Now that this has happened to me, what am I going to do about it?" (p. 136)

On reading these words, I wondered how a Christian spirituality might impact them. Is there a Christian perspective that might enlarge the interpretative framework needed to figure these things out and decisively respond to the what-am-I-going-to-do-about-it question?

From my Christian point of view, I wondered whether some "bad things" might not "have a meaning" when they happen. (The crucifixion of Jesus comes to mind.) Such events could indeed be accepted willingly for a very good theological reason. There is, of course, an unacceptable reason that I would dismiss along with Rabbi Kushner, namely, that something someone did makes him or her "deserve" this truly horrific outcome. That kind of thinking turns God into a mean-spirited umpire anxious to call you "out" at the plate, instead of waiting, like the father of the prodigal son in the parable in Luke's Gospel, to welcome you home.

Both Jewish and Christian spirituality are careful not to put the blame on God when reversals occur. So-called acts of God are really acts of nature. It is true, of course, that God is the Creator of all things natural, but nature's laws—the law of gravity, for example—play themselves out without divine interference. Kushner is particularly good on this point, refusing as he does to blame God for the agony of a cancer patient, but insisting at the same time that the action of God is clearly visible in the "gifts" bestowed on such patients: "the strength to take each day as it comes, to be grateful for a day full of sunshine or one in which they are relatively free of pain."

According to Kushner, the vexing questions that enter the lives of those who find the world closing in on them—the victims of disease or downsizing, the survivors who mourn the death of a spouse or child—will surface in every life and recur in every generation. "The questions never change," he observes; "the search for a satisfying answer continues." That is where I found myself pausing as I read this insightful book—a book I readily recommend to anyone burdened with tragedy and distress—and coming to a different conclusion, one that I had the opportunity to mention to Rabbi Kushner in a conversation we had early in 1997.

For me, and for those who believe as I do, the search has ended in Christ. This is not to say that I, or we, or anyone else "has all the answers." I mean only to say that the reflective Christian has met Christ as a serious questioner meets a satisfying answer. Christian spirituality savors the satisfaction of the answer in a challenging, but never complacent, way. The challenge is what Christians call the Paschal Mystery, an intriguing notion to be explored below.

Any person of faith, Jew or Christian, can agree with Kushner's observation that the success in your search for answers depends greatly on what you mean by "answer." If you expect fully satisfying explanations, there is "probably no satisfying answer." The pain "will still be there."

But so will you still be there. And life will be there challenging you to get on with it, to face up to the future, to help others, to love and smile and grow, and to believe that God is there with you, right there at your side. "That's the spirit," you might find yourself saying to someone else who is trying in this way to rebound bravely and recover from a shattering reversal.

The "spirit" you admire is, in fact, a functioning spirituality; it is evidence of the presence of the Holy Spirit in the human soul.

The underlying spirituality of this book equips you with some admittedly soft solutions to life's hard problems and provides you with *invisible* means of support. You may try it out, as Peter tried walking on the water (Matt 14:28–31), only to lose heart and begin to sink, or you may adopt the spiritual solutions as forces that imperceptibly supply balance, coherence, and consistency to all that you do.

Peter's problem related to shaky faith. He and a boat full of disciples of Jesus were quite a distance from shore on a windy night in very choppy waters. Matthew's Gospel recounts that Jesus came toward them walking on the water. When the disciples saw him walking on the water they were terrified, but Jesus said to them, "Take heart, it is I; do not be afraid" (Matt 14:27). He then invited Peter to come toward him—to walk on the waves. As the Gospel account relates, "Peter got out of the boat, started walking on the water, and came toward Jesus" (v. 29). For the moment, Peter's faith sustained him. But when he saw how strong the wind and the waves were, he faltered, began to sink, and cried for help. And the Gospel account, in words that have found their way into the hearts of Christians, says, "Jesus immediately reached out his hand and caught him, saying to him, 'You of little faith, why did you doubt?'" (v. 31).

Belief in Jesus as Son of God and the Messiah sets Christians apart from Jews; it is a fundamental difference between the faiths. And the difference lies not simply in an assent, on the part of Christians, to the proposition that Jesus is divine. It is more complex. The difference lies in a spirituality that integrates, however incompletely, the dimensions of the so-called paschal mystery.

This expression encompasses the reality of Easter—the sufferings, death, resurrection, and ascension of Jesus. The paschal mystery enables the eye of Christian faith to "see" that there is life through death, a notion that is rooted in the Hebrew Scriptures that relate the story of the original *Pasch* or "Passover." The paschal mystery provides an interpretative framework wherein the Christian comes to believe that the route to glory passes through shame and humiliation. In this faith-based value system, loss is the price of gain; defeat is the preface to victory. For those who believe this, personal hardships—including those encountered on the job—do, in fact, have meaning, and transcendent meaning at that.

This specifically Christian perspective raises a host of intriguing issues. For example, in his book *Why Work*, Michael Maccoby plays on Lord Acton's famous saying, "Power tends to corrupt, and absolute power tends to corrupt absolutely." Maccoby offers as a corollary to Acton's dictum, "The equally certain law that power-lessness perverts" (p. 67). Christians, however, have a basis in faith for not overlooking the power of power-lessness.

Dealing with difficulties at any stage and place in life can be a spiritual exercise, one that adds meaning to life. Just as the Father raised Jesus from the dead, the Christian's Easter faith would maintain, so those whose baptism "plunged" them sacramentally and symboli-cally into the death of Jesus will also rise with Jesus to eternal glory. The process begins with baptism, which enables the baptized to "die" symbolically with Jesus and then "rise" to walk in "newness of life" (the life of grace). In that "death" is found a faith-based reality that puts the sorrows and setbacks of life into proper per-spective, where they become preludes to glory.

Belief in the resurrection of Jesus is central to the Christian faith. To try to figure out exactly how that event happened is to reduce a mystery to a problem to be solved. The only "solution" is faith, the faith that enables Christians to make sense out of pain, suffering, illness, disappointment, defeat, and death. They know, by faith, that "resurrection" recoveries are available to them, by God's grace, in the aftermath of any rever-sal on their journey through life. They eventually die knowing that, again by God's grace, they will rise from death to eternal life.

Knowing all this by faith, Christians find themselves at Easter time singing *Amazing Grace* and giving thanks to God in Christ for making their redemption possible. If all this is true, then this life with all its difficulties is something tremendously worth living to the full. Surely, it has its ups and downs, but all of it—pain and gain, sorrow and joy, defeat and victory—is good precisely because God chose to make it so in Christ.

So, when bad things happen to good Christians, they are able to call upon their own interpretative framework to search for a deeper meaning, a meaning that is available only to the eye of faith. This is not a grin-and-bear-it exercise, or a matter of "carrying your cross." The meaning derives from a quiet conviction that the glorified Jesus, the victorious Jesus, lives now in glory. He is an eternal "winner" who is at the side of every believer at every stage of the believer's life. Christ's victory, in short, can never be reversed. And therein lies the basis for the Christian believer's hope.

There is no room for smug complacency here. It is not that you have picked a winner, but that a winner has picked you. All that you can do is be grateful and remain faithful. And remaining faithful requires you to act according to the law of love.

Let me close this circle—that opened with an excerpt from Rabbi Kushner's book—by recalling the words of the prophet Micah, words that are applicable today, of course, to both Christians and Jews:

He has told you, O mortal, what is good;
  and what does the LORD require of you
but to do justice, and to love kindness,
  and to walk humbly with your God?
    (Mic 6:8)

That sounds like the basis of a spirituality capable of transforming persons in a world where bad things can happen to anyone, but where everyone can survive and even prosper by simply choosing to "walk humbly with your God."

7

Hope

As noted earlier, the poet George Herbert expressed the encouraging idea that anyone "who walks in hope dances without music." Growing old gratefully means walking in hope as you progress through the years.

Hope is the best route into the retirement years. Remember, hope is a theological virtue; its object is God. Forge that link for yourself in prayer and everything else will fall into line.

Never forget that you can make the God in whom you hope become present for others wherever you are simply by being hopeful. Your centered hopefulness (a quality not to be confused with blind, Pollyanna-inspired optimism) makes you an anchor, a rock for others, a source of serenity and stability. And, as is always the case in the realm of Christian spirituality, in providing this kind of help to others, you are also helping yourself.

This phenomenon may exemplify what the French novelist George Bernanos called "the miracle of the empty hands." You, who stand in need of hope, can give it to others without necessarily feeling very hopeful yourself. And so it is with love, faith, trust, and forgiveness: you can give what you think you do not have. In the realm of spirituality, at any rate, you can; this should serve to remind us where the power is, and has been, all along. I knew a wonderful priest who was fond of saying, "Jesus promises you two things: your life will have meaning, and you're going to live forever. If you can find a better offer, take it." Build your future on the durability of hope.

Hope is the pillar of the world. Because of it, you are stronger than you think. It may surprise you to learn that John Updike once wrote, "God is a bottomless encouragement to our faltering and frightened being." It may not surprise you to know that St. Paul said much the same thing centuries earlier: "We also boast in our sufferings, knowing that suffering produces endurance, and endurance produces character, and character produces hope, and hope does not disappoint us, because God's love has been poured into our hearts through the Holy Spirit that has been given to us" (Rom 5:3–5).

Your hope will surely never disappoint if the object of your hope is God. When your hopes appear to be "dashed," consider the possibility that the God in whom you never stop hoping has something better in mind for you.

Hope is always future-focused. It fuels your second starts. It sustains your journey through life, especially through life's final stages. Knowing, as you do, that "all the world's a stage," you should acknowledge your potential (even propensity) to "act," and check the face behind your mask. Are you smiling? Are you truly a hopeful person?

What abiding hope can do for you was demonstrated beautifully by Cardinal Joseph Bernardin as his life ended in November 1996. "His way of death confirms that this man did not have two faces, one private, one public," said Rabbi Herman Schaalman, a longtime friend. "He was inside with his outside, outside with his inside, which is rare."

That rare quality is the fruit of a functioning spirituality. The ultimate answers come from within because your spiritual guidelines long ago found root there. Your inside becomes your outside in moments of challenge; you can face reality without losing either heart or hope.

The memorial card distributed to those who paid their respects at the wake service and funeral held in Chicago for Cardinal Bernardin had his picture on the front and the "Prayer of St. Francis" on the back. The Cardinal carried that prayer in his coat pocket every day and recited it often. "Lord, make me an instrument of your peace," is the opening petition; midway through a list of subsequent requests, you will find these words: "Where there is despair, let me sow hope." Every believer wants to do just that.

Take to heart these words from Simon Peter, the first pope: "Always be ready to make your defense to anyone who demands from you an accounting for the hope that is in you" (1 Pet 3:15). He presumed, apparently, that the Christian believer would always be a puzzle to the world. Truth be told, if you are genuinely hopeful, you will puzzle many even today.

8

Psalm Stops

Pausing occasionally to ponder a psalm is a helpful process of growing old gratefully. I like to think of "psalm stops" along the way home to heaven. The point is to pause and to listen. God speaks; you respond. You don't hear the words; you read them prayerfully. You know that they are inspired words, so you read them reverently. And you let them sink into your soul. As the Letter to the Hebrews states, "The word of God is living and active, sharper than any two-edged sword, piercing until it divides soul from spirit, joints from marrow; it is able to judge the thoughts and intentions of the heart" (Heb 4:12). That's your soul and spirit, your joints and marrow, so at every "psalm stop" just let the words sink in to whatever it is that constitutes your self.

Everyone has some favorite psalms or psalm phrases. Listed below are lines lifted from the Book of

Psalms. They are there for your pondering. Of course, you can search all the psalms for other phrases that appeal to you. In the spirit of this book, you may want to search out the psalms that stress the notion of gratitude. In any case, here is a sampling:

> *The promise of the LORD proves true; / he is a shield for all who take refuge in him* (Ps 18:30). God stands by his promise; we live by it. We live surrounded and shielded by God's love. Trust is another word for faith. Those who "trust in him" live by faith and thus live securely.

> *The LORD is my shepherd, I shall not want* (Ps 23:1). This is a popular psalm but not everyone really believes what it says. Again, it takes faith to see the shepherd by your side and even more faith to follow faithfully wherever your shepherd leads.

> *The LORD is my light and my salvation; / whom shall I fear?* (Ps 27:1). Who or what do you fear? Name them. Each fear adds a dimension of darkness to your life; your fears crowd out the Lord who is your light. So, let the Lord in, let the Lord shine, and let that light drive out the darkness. Just let it be. Let it happen.

Wait for the LORD; / be strong, and let your heart take courage; / wait for the LORD! (Ps 27:14). These words will be all you need at times to revive your sinking spirits. We can easily lose heart; waiting is the key to acquisition of stoutheartedness, but it will come only if you wait for the Lord.

Sing praises to the LORD, O you his faithful ones, / and give thanks to his holy name. / For his anger is but for a moment; / his favor is for a lifetime (Ps 30:4–5). There it is, plain and simple—a reason for gratitude.

Happy are those whose transgression is forgiven, / whose sin is covered (Ps 32:1). Forgiveness means removal. The fault is gone—forever. How then can you not be happy and grateful? But without faith, the acceptance of forgiveness is a challenge. Faith and forgiveness are two sides of the same coin, the coin that we call mercy.

The LORD looks down from heaven; / he sees all humankind. / From where he sits enthroned he watches / all the inhabitants of the earth— / he who fashions the hearts of them all, / and observes all their deeds (Ps 33:13–15). You are known and seen by the Lord. The "Great Surveyor" fashioned your heart and measures your works. The

Lord is looking down on you from heaven, not to "check up," but only to be watchful, faithful, and protective, to give you credit for your progress and to catch you if you fall. So, look up and know that the Lord is there; look ahead and move wherever your Lord prompts you to go.

He alone is my rock and my salvation, / my fortress; I shall never be shaken (Ps 62:2). Single-hearted conviction—you shall never fall, never waver, never be alone because your soul rests in God. You know you have to act. You have to do, not simply be. But you also know that when you act, it is God acting in you. You shall never really fall.

For as the heavens are high above the earth, / so great is his steadfast love toward those who fear him; / as far as the east is from the west, / so far he removes our transgressions from us (Ps 103:11–12). Here you have the dimensions of God's mercy and you simply have to believe that all your guilt is buried there. That's where your guilt belongs. Never permit it to return to trouble you. Always be grateful that it has been removed.

O LORD, you have searched me and known me. / You know when I sit down and when I rise up; / you discern my thoughts from far away (Ps 139:1–2). Far is not far where the Lord is concerned. You are known from within, no matter where you happen to be. You cannot not be known by the Lord, who holds your destiny in his loving hands.

In your reflection, continue to comb through the psalms, lift a line or two here and there—any line that speaks to you—and listen quietly.

9

Of Wars and Remembrance

Catholic Christians are a remembering people. We remember the Lord "in the breaking of the bread." We remember our past in art and architecture, in the lives of our saints, in the history of missionary activity, ecumenical councils, and so much more. Remembering is part of who we are. And good memories are very much a part of growing old gratefully.

So, it is quite congenial for us to participate each year in our nation's Memorial Day celebration, the civic remembrance of those who fought and died in military service. Even those among us who are opposed to war are open to prayer and reflection prompted by this annual day of remembrance at the end of May.

In 2005, as the nation marked the sixtieth anniversary in early May of the end of our war with Nazi Germany, Baltimore Catholics were pleased to read in their daily newspaper the story of the bravery of their retired Archbishop William Donald Borders. Many were unaware that he saw combat duty as a chaplain in World War II. The *Baltimore Sun* reporter coaxed out of him some of the details of the heroic action that won for him the Bronze Star for Valor.

He was a battalion chaplain, not quite 30 years old, with the 91st Infantry Division in Italy in September 1944. During an attack on a German position, one of the American troops was hit and lay wounded on the battlefield. Chaplain Borders ran out under machine-gun fire, lifted the fallen soldier to his shoulder, and moved him to safety. "After I anointed him, they sent him to the rear and I never saw him again," the retired archbishop told the reporter.

When asked about bravery in the face of danger, the Archbishop replied, "It didn't enter your mind one way or another, you're too busy. You're involved all the time. When you're involved, you're thinking about what you're doing, not: am I brave, or am I not brave. It just doesn't enter your mind. Another person says you're courageous. You don't think of it. The motivation is somebody needs help, pure and simple."

Then 91, Archbishop Borders had been helping people in a variety of circumstances and in many places over the years. "Nobody prepares you for battle," Archbishop Borders said to the reporter. "You can't do it. How do you prepare for someone dying?"

What did he do on the battlefield? "If they were conscious, I talked to them, gave them counsel, administered the sacraments of penance and the Holy Eucharist, and anointed many people who were dying. I don't have any idea how many. You don't keep statistics. It wasn't constant, of course. Combat is never constant. It comes and goes."

With the help of the annual Washington, DC, Memorial Day Concert, seen live or on public television from the West Lawn of the Capitol on the Sunday evening before the Memorial Day holiday, millions of Americans can understand what Archbishop Borders meant when he closed out the newspaper interview by saying softly, "It was a long time ago, but you never forget something like that."

Catholics across the nation, not just in Baltimore, are both humbly proud and proudly humble to have been served by the likes of William Donald Borders, who reached out for so many years simply because "somebody needs help." Without realizing it, he set a fitting example for anyone to follow who wants to grow old gratefully.

10

The Oxygen of Affirmation

On February 10, 2005, the death of Arthur Miller, at age 89, triggered an outpouring of praise for one of America's greatest playwrights. His 1949 classic, "Death of a Salesman," is the only work I'll mention here. His creation of Willy Lowman, the salesman who needed the oxygen of affirmation, and Willy's wife, Linda, whose words provided it so movingly but unsuccessfully, was Miller's great contribution to our national treasury of dramatic memory.

We need great plays to help us better understand ourselves, to see our failures and regrets, and to learn how we might change as well as stay the course on our voyage through the years.

Linda Lowman, aware of Willy's downward spiral of discouragement and eroding self-confidence, pleads with their two sons, Happy and Biff, to show their father more respect. "He's the dearest man in the world to me," she says, "and I won't have anyone making him feel unwanted and low and blue." Biff tells her to "stop making excuses for him" and cruelly adds that Willy never respected her. Linda replies, "Biff, I don't say he's a great man. Willy Lowman never made a lot of money. His name was never in the paper. He's not the finest character that ever lived. But he's a human being, and a terrible thing is happening to him. So attention must be paid. He's not to be allowed to fall into his grave like an old dog. Attention, attention must be finally paid to such a person."

Linda then urges her son to "be sweet to him tonight, dear. Be loving to him. Because he's only a little boat looking for a harbor."

Miller was 33 when "Death of a Salesman" opened on Broadway. At age 68, he said in an interview with the *New York Times* that he could see himself in the character of Willy Lowman, although when the play opened he tended to identify more with Willy's son Biff. But now, "When Biff's yelling at Willy, he's yelling at me. I understand Willy. And I understand his longing for immortality—I think that's inevitable when you get older….Willy's writing his name on a cake of ice on a hot day, but he wishes he were writing in stone. He wants to live on through something....I think all of us want that, and it gets more poignant as we get more anonymous in the world."

Willy believed "a man has got to add up to something." He couldn't face living the rest of his life "ringing up a zero." Early in the play, Willy says, "You're my foundation and support, Linda." But eventually he takes his own life. At his graveside, neighbor Charley says to Biff, "Willy was a salesman. And for a salesman, there is no rock bottom to the life. He don't put a bolt to a nut, he don't tell you the law or give you medicine. He's a man way out there in the blue, riding on a smile and a shoeshine. And when they start not smiling back— that's an earthquake. And then you get yourself a couple of spots on your hat, and you're finished. Nobody dast blame this man. A salesman is got to dream, boy. It comes with the territory."

Our world is full of Willys, writing their names on cakes of ice. They need the gently heroic Lindas for support and encouragement. And all of us Willys and Lindas can be grateful to Arthur Miller for the spirit-sustaining insights that his genius left behind.

11

A Road Map

Pope Benedict XVI was speaking to about 25,000 seminarians and young people on the next-to-last day of his six-day visit to the United States in 2008 when he said, "Walking in the Lord's footsteps, our own lives become a journey of hope." He might just as well have had all Christians in mind as he mapped out this path of discipleship. What a beautiful way to think of our lives as the years mount up—a journey of hope.

The Holy Father began by recalling that St. Peter urged all Christians to "proclaim the Lord Christ" and to "be ready to make your defense to anyone who demands from you an accounting for the hope that is in you" (1 Pet 3:15). So, this successor of Peter took the occasion to repeat St. Peter's challenge and "share with you some thoughts about being disciples of Jesus Christ." Benedict described discipleship as "walking in the Lord's footsteps." Take that walk, he said, and your life becomes "a journey of hope."

Twice in the talk, Benedict urged his hearers to offer "an outstretched hand of hope" to those they meet along the way and by that simple gesture perhaps "awakening in them a life of faith." After recalling that his own teenage years "were marred by a sinister regime" (Nazism in Germany) that was eventually "recognized for the monster it was," he went on to say that the "power to destroy...never triumphs." We recall this most dramatically, he said, in the season of Easter, and he noted that the conviction that the power to destroy never triumphs "is the essence of the hope that defines us as Christians."

Unbelievers have first to see some signs of hope before they will be prompted to ask, as St. Peter said they would, about "the reason for the hope that is within you." By making the "hand of hope" visible in our time, we Christians can, in Pope Benedict's view, help to dispel the darkness of heart and mind in our world.

That darkness sets in, he said, "when people, especially the most vulnerable, encounter a clenched fist of repression or manipulation rather than a hand of hope." He had in mind those "affected by drug and substance abuse, homelessness and poverty, racism, violence, and degradation—especially of girls and women." Acknowledging that the causes of these problems are "complex," Pope Benedict said they are rooted in "a poisoned attitude of mind" and a certain "callousness of heart." "Such tragedies also point to what might have been and what could be, were there other hands—your hands— reaching out."

"We are tempted to close in on ourselves, to doubt the strength of Christ's radiance, to limit the horizon of hope. Take courage!…Let your imaginations soar freely along the limitless expanse of the horizons of Christian discipleship." And then he outlined a road map for discipleship by calling attention to "four essential aspects of the treasure of our faith: personal prayer and silence, liturgical prayer, charity in action, and vocations."

In personal prayer and silence, you can hear God's call, he said. You can "look about you with Christ's eyes, listen with his ears, feel and think with his heart and mind." Out of this prayer, "hope in action" can emerge. Putting it bluntly, Pope Benedict asked the young, "Are you ready to give all, as he did, for truth and justice?"

Liturgical prayer brings you "closer to God and also prepares you to serve others;" it prepares you for "charity in action." When he turned to vocations, Benedict first praised "the vocation of marriage and family life," and then urged consideration of the call to priesthood and religious life. In responding to your call, he said, "Remember that what counts before the Lord is to dwell in his love and to make his love shine forth for others."

12

Happy 80th Birthday, Papa

Reverence for ancestors is an admirable thread in Chinese culture. It was wonderful to see that thread running through an 80th birthday celebration for retired neurosurgeon Paul Lin, who was born in China, left at age 22 when the Communists took control, and came to Philadelphia for his neurosurgical residency and subsequent medical career. He married an Italian-American nurse and raised a family of six. Friends and family gathered for a midday, full-course Sunday meal in one of Philadelphia's suburban Chinese restaurants, closed to the public for this special birthday celebration.

Memories were recalled for the grandchildren throughout the meal in visual and story form. The kids produced memories of their own by reading personalized tributes to "Papa." A central theme that ran through their admiring words was an expression of gratitude for Papa's quiet presence to and with them. He was there for their recitals, performances, and games. He was there, said one, "when I would build with Legos and he would watch the news or golf on TV, and we felt no need to speak or engage in superfluous chitchat. Every half hour or so, we would look up, make eye contact, and then go back to our separate pursuits....I still enjoy sitting on the couch and reading with Papa, with or without conversation," she said. "I've always admired and respected my grandfather's intellectual gifts and his appreciation for silence."

An absent granddaughter (away volunteering with a medical missionary unit in Bangladesh) sent a message recalling that "Papa reminds us how in China, one does not wither away as the years pile up; rather, one gains respect, honor, and knowledge. He jokingly suggested to me once that we start calling him 'The Venerable.' So, Venerable Papa, Happy Birthday; you are one year wiser. I love you!"

Several of the youngsters expressed gratitude for his persistence in putting vocabulary-builders in their hands in attractive tapes, books, and word game formats. "Papa has always wanted all the young kids to succeed in school. He always asks how our grades are and how school is going."

Papa also came to the rescue in creative ways. "My

fondest memory of Papa is when he saved my stuffed animal Free Willy. As a child, I loved stuffed animals. On our family trip to Florida, I received a stuffed animal whale and named it Free Willy. I took him everywhere. One day I had left him around and Moe, our dog, tore him to shreds. I was crushed. I felt as if my friend had died. The grown-ups, not knowing what to do with this bawling kid, quietly got out Papa's surgical kit. I patiently watched Papa sew my baby back together. I honestly believed he was doing surgery on my stuffed animal! Even though I've given away most of my animals, I will always keep Free Willy."

And another child wrote, "I broke a board with my elbow at Karate. Papa knew that I liked Chinese characters, so he took one of the boards and painted 'Merry Christmas' on it for me. We hung the board on a wall in my bedroom. Thank you, Papa. That board will always be very special to me."

More memories of the fishing pier on the New Jersey Shore, trips to the penny arcade, boardwalk breakfasts, first-ever swings with a golf club, a "contract" to a would-be filmmaker to make a documentary for his grandparents' fiftieth wedding anniversary based on interviews and old photo montages but without a word about this to his grandmother. "Now he calls me, 'Mr. Spielberg,'" says this proud grandson of a perfect Papa!

As I write, Papa, now 90, lives on—feeble but deeply content. He knows he has much for which to be grateful. Without intending it, he is enabling his children and grandchildren to discover the importance of gratitude in their lives.

His daughter Jennifer, a retired reporter with the *Philadelphia Inquirer*, has dedicated her book, *Shanghai Faithful: Betrayal and Forgiveness in a Chinese Christian Family*, to him. It is a remarkable narrative covering five generations of the Lin family. Her father called the project her "obsession," and he was right. It started when she wrote two stories about China as a summer intern for the *Bucks County Courier Times* in 1979, and continued through a residency in China with her husband and two children in the 1990s. The central figure in the book is Jennifer's grandfather, Paul's father, Lin Pu-chi, an Anglican priest, who had studied in the United States and was resourceful enough to get his youngest son Paul and Paul's elder brother Tim out of China just as the Cultural Revolution was beginning. The Lin family is exemplary for "keeping the faith" and remaining ever grateful. And Jennifer is to be admired for using her talent to preserve special, sometimes painful, memories of a special family.

Paul Lin died at the age of 91 on August 13, 2017.

13

Your Epitaph

Benjamin Franklin wrote his epitaph when he was only 28. Most of us never get around to putting an epitaph together although we often think of phrases that could nicely summarize our lives. W.C. Fields is famous for his unkind cut: "Better Here than in Philadelphia." Franklin, a Philadelphia original, set a positive, high, and serious standard for an epitaph with these words:

The Body of
B Franklin Printer,
(Like the Cover of an old Book
Its Contents torn out
And stript of its Lettering and Gilding)
Lies here, Food for Worms.
But the Work shall not be lost;
For it will, (as he believ'd) appear once more,

In a new and more elegant Edition
Revised and Corrected,
By the Author.

What an original way to think of the resurrection of the body, which is, of course, a central truth of the Christian faith. I often think, as I drive past a cemetery or participate in a burial ceremony, of what that "new and more elegant edition" will look like on the last day. I think of all those bodies rising again and being clothed in white robes standing by their empty graves. I speculate that no matter what age we are when we die, our bodies will be about 33 years of age when they rise again on the last day. That's an age that matches the prime of life. It is also the age of Jesus when he died and rose again. This, of course, is pure speculation; we have no way of knowing for sure; we can only speculate. We do, however, know by faith, and therefore with certainty, that we will rise again, body and soul, and live for all eternity. Speculating on what that life will be like—no pain, no hunger, no thirst, no diminishment, no fatigue—is a nice accompaniment to the growing-old years.

Thinking about how you would like to be remembered is a healthy exercise. Rather than trying to compose an epitaph, you might want to try your hand at an obituary. That gives you more space, a fuller range for remembrance and reflection. And it will surely generate a lengthy list of persons to be thanked now, while it is not too late.

My friend who was fond of giving a round wooden ring to others and telling them that it was a "round tuit," confessed that he handed them out because he always wanted to say thanks but found that he "never got around to it." We just never get around to doing those minor things that make life richer for others and also for ourselves. The Book of Proverbs has a wise saying— "Better is open rebuke than hidden love" (Prov 27:5). Give voice to those good thoughts and feelings and you will find yourself building a better world.

Your speculation on the afterlife tells you that there will surely be voices there. What about languages? You will understand them all and others will understand you; somehow or other the language of love will certainly touch everyone.

You may not be in the mood just now to try your hand at writing an epitaph or obituary; that is quite understandable and no cause for concern. But don't pass up the opportunity to compose a thank you list, and be sure to turn to it in prayer every now and then.

Meanwhile, take a sober assessment of your environment. Look at what you see and know to be part of your surroundings. Most, if not all of it, you can surely say, will outlast me; but, you can say just as surely, none of this is going to outlive me. You are going to live forever. You can count on it. And all you can be is grateful.

14

Considering
"The Alternative"

One of my friends typically conveys news of someone's death by remarking that the deceased person "has joined the majority." Another friend likes to say, "He rolled a seven," when reporting that someone we both knew has died.

Deaths of celebrities reported in the daily news can have the effect of forcing people to think about, if not face up to, the inevitability of their own deaths. Few of us are famous for doing that.

I remember speaking to a woman who was well on the road to recovery after a serious illness and she said, "I'm doing just fine now, considering the alternative." "But did you ever really consider the alternative?"

I asked. She smiled and said, "I guess I should." And so should we all, as we elder along in life.

"What no eye has seen, nor ear heard, / nor the human heart conceived, / what God has prepared for those who love him" (1 Cor 2:9). Those words are part of divine revelation. That's God speaking to each one of us. But we refuse to listen in faith. We refuse to permit ourselves positively and hopefully to "consider the alternative."

In the book *Life, Death, and Christian Hope*, Daneen Warner reflects on the meaning of hope in the context of death. She notes that because they fail to see their own death in the light of Christ's death and resurrection, many Christians "place their faith and hope in medicine" and thus "harbor a false sense of security concerning their mortality."

If you really believe in the resurrection of Christ, death is already behind you. "Death's not what we're moving toward," as Father Clarence Rivers said many years ago, "it's what we're coming from!" The challenge for us, as Daneen Warner explains, is to face up to our cultural bias against accepting the fact that death is an inevitable part of life, by "shifting our hope in human powers to hope in God." That means taking it on faith that the death and resurrection of Jesus have overcome death for all who believe in Jesus.

Have the courage now to think out loud once in a while about what it will be like when you "join the majority." That's another way of saying "consider the alternative." A hymn that is part of Night Prayer in the Liturgy of the Hours (the Divine Office or Breviary, as it is sometimes called) says it well:

> We praise you, Father, for your gifts
> Of dusk and nightfall over earth,
> Foreshadowing the mystery
> of death that leads to endless day.

You are going to experience "endless day" once you "join the majority." You are going to be eternally awake and eternally aware. The English word *enthusiasm* comes from two Greek words, *en theos*, meaning "in God." That will be your experience. You might start thinking now of what eternal enthusiasm will be like for you. And think of the generations that have gone on before. You will meet them all. You will know the saints to whom you prayed, the historical figures you admired, and billions of others whom you never knew existed, and you will be reunited with those you loved the most when they shared space and life with you on this earth. They will all be part of your eternal awareness. As will the mysteries of faith and the "mysteries" of things like calculus and chemistry that you never managed to translate from textbook print to mental assimilation.

Go ahead now and see if you can let yourself say, "I can hardly wait!"

15

"Death's Not What We're Moving Toward; It's What We're Coming From"

This line that we quoted in the last chapter from the late African-American priest-composer Clarence Rivers is a mantra worth repeating often and gratefully by any person of faith who is eldering along toward the end of life. In the view of the world, you are moving toward a place on the obituary pages. To the eye of faith, life is out there in front waiting to welcome you.

For you, death was buried in the resurrection of Jesus. Resurrection is a new beginning. In the wake of the resurrection, Jesus experienced an ascension into heaven where his new beginning puts him in what can be seen correctly as a judgment seat but that can also be viewed as a welcoming posture with arms outstretched and ready to embrace the forgiven and faithful follower. Reflect on the words, "Death's not what I'm moving toward; it's what I'm coming from."

Some years ago, I began thinking of doorways as passage points, as entryways. Moving through, I would encourage myself to say, "through death to life," and I would imagine the outstretched arms of Christ—extended on the cross—now free of the nails and, in a glorified state, wrapping themselves around me in an embrace of welcome. This is never a morbid exercise. It is a walking act of faith, hope, and love. It happens at home, of course, but it can happen anywhere at any time. Wherever there is a doorway, there is a reminder of the life to come and the eternal embrace that is waiting there. In recent years, I also began to think of how the words of consecration at Mass, specifically the words spoken by the priest over the wine, suggest a plan of life for the believer. "In a similar way, when supper was ended, he took the chalice. And once more giving thanks said, 'Take this, all of you, and drink from it. For this is the chalice of my blood, the blood of the new and eternal covenant, which will be poured out for you and for many, for the forgiveness of sins. Do this in memory of me.'"

The "poured-out life" is not only a beautiful description of the life of Christ but is a blueprint for the life of anyone who wants to be a follower of Christ. We don't simply remember; we follow. And the following involves permitting ourselves to be "broken" open and passed around for the nourishment of others, as Christ was broken open for our salvation and is now bread broken and passed around in every Mass. And we follow Christ by permitting ourselves to be "poured out" in service to others, as Christ was poured out for us in his life, death, and resurrection.

We celebrate and give thanks at every Mass. Good liturgy means giving praise gratefully. And there at the table of the Eucharist, we take needed nourishment to sustain us in our faith journey, which is a journey of generous service to others. That's why we can say (and sing) along with Clarence Rivers, that "Death's not what we're moving toward; it's what we're coming from!"

About the Author

Jesuit Father William J. Byron is a retired university professor of business and society at St. Joseph's University, Philadelphia, Pennsylvania. He is past president of the University of Scranton (1975–82), the Catholic University of America (1982–92), Loyola University of New Orleans (2003–4), and served as interim president of St. Joseph's Preparatory School in Philadelphia from 2006 to 2008. He was director of Georgetown University's Center for the Advanced Study of Ethics (1994–97) and taught courses on the social responsibilities of business in the McDonough School of Business at Georgetown. An Army paratrooper from 1945 to 1946, he holds a bachelor's degree and licentiate in philosophy, and a master's in economics from St. Louis University, a bachelor's and licentiate in theology from Woodstock College, and a doctorate in economics from the University of Maryland. He is the author of twenty-one books and editor of two, and the recipient of thirty honorary degrees. For sixteen years, Father Byron wrote a biweekly general interest column called "Looking Around" for the Catholic News Service Syndicate.